100 YEARS OF FOOTBALL

To The Bauman's,

This is PROPER FOOTBALL!

Take Care,

Sean

L.F.C.
crown paints

100 YEARS OF FOOTBALL

PA Photos

AMMONITE
PRESS

First published 2008 by

AMMONITE PRESS

an imprint of AE Publications Ltd,

166 High Street, Lewes, East Sussex BN7 1XU

ISBN 978-1-906672-01-0

British Cataloguing in Publication Data. A catalogue record of this book is available from the British Library.

Editor **NEIL DUNNICLIFFE**

Designer **JO PATTERSON**

Colour origination by GMC Reprographics

Printed and bound by Colorprint Offset in China

Contents

JVC

Chapter One

PEOPLE

THE GREAT AND GOOD

For all the epic competitions it is the big personalities that make football such an enthralling game.

Giants of the old English Division One included Steve Bloomer, a striker who notched up an impressive 314 goals in 534 matches. Giant goal-keeper William Foulke weighed 25 stone and was the antithesis of today's ultra slim players, but no less effective. Billy Meredith left his mining roots behind to play for Manchester City. He scored both goals for City in the first Manchester derby, went on to play for Manchester United and turned out in the FA Cup aged 49.

THE 1910s TO THE 1950s

Dixie, or William, Dean became the most prolific scorer in English history. He averaged a goal a game, even more for his country. Ted Drake is remembered as the first man to win the Division One title as both player and manager, but also as a lethal finisher, netting 44 goals in one season for Arsenal as well as seven in one match.

Hughie Gallacher rose through the Scottish ranks and became perhaps

RIGHT BILL 'FATTY' FOULKE, CHELSEA GOALKEEPER. 11/09/1905

FAR RIGHT BILL 'DIXIE' DEAN, EVERTON. 26/09/1931

Newcastle United's finest ever player, netting 143 times. Danny Blanchflower was inspirational for both his clubs and Northern Ireland. John Charles starred for Wales, Leeds, Cardiff, Juventus and Roma.

Sir Matt Busby crossed the divides by playing for both Manchester clubs, Liverpool and his country; going on to manage Manchester United to five league titles and the European Cup. Other successful players of the time included Sir Stanley Matthews, Nat Lofthouse and Billy Wright.

SWINGING SIXTIES

The 1960s were the biggest decade yet for English football due in no small part to England's famous World Cup win in 1966.
The whole of the England team and its manager Sir Alf Ramsey are venerated as heroes to this day. In the annals of English football the likes of goalkeeper Gordon Banks, midfield battler Alan Ball, brothers Sir Jack Charlton and Sir Bobby Charlton and the scorer of a hat-trick in the final, Sir Geoff Hurst are legendary.

A year later Glasgow Celtic became the first UK club to win the European Cup by beating Inter Milan 2-1 in the final with Tommy Gemmell netting a spectacular winner. Glasgow Rangers responded by winning the Cup Winners' Cup in 1972 led by captain John Greig. Denis Law played for Manchester City, before helping Manchester United to win the European Cup in 1968.

Bill Shankly spent 15 years at the helm of Liverpool bringing them a trio of First Division titles, two FA Cups and the UEFA Cup.

Jimmy Greaves was devastated to miss most of England's 1966 World Cup triumph, but his glittering career saw him hit the net 357 times in 516 First Division games with 44 goals in his 57 internationals. George Best, one of the wildest spirits the game has ever seen, was also one of its most supreme talents, playing for Manchester United, Northern Ireland, Hibernian and Fulham. He was one of the first real superstars of UK football.

SEVENTIES STARS

The 1970s saw English football really take off as Liverpool snared the European Cup in 1977 and 1978, followed in 1979 by Brian Clough's Nottingham Forest. Clough was arguably the greatest manager of the decade, bringing a no-nonsense attitude to management.

The decade also saw two legends emerge at the other end of the pitch – in Pat Jennings and Peter Shilton. Jennings was perhaps Northern

PETER SHILTON, LEICESTER CITY GOALKEEPER. 23/03/1968

LEFT
ENGLAND'S GARY LINEKER SCORES THE SECOND GOAL OF A HAT-TRICK. 11/06/1986

Ireland's greatest ever goalkeeper as well as being eulogised by the fans of both London rivals Arsenal and Tottenham Hotspur. Shilton meanwhile starred for England and a host of English club sides, winning two European Cups with Nottingham Forest and becoming the first player to make 1,000 professional appearances in England.

Bob Paisley filled the big shoes of Shankly at Liverpool by taking the club to three European Cups and six First Division championships. Essential to his success were his brace of Scots, Alan Hansen and Kenny Dalglish. Another key striker was Englishman Kevin Keegan, who turned out for Liverpool before moving to Hamburg.

EIGHTIES HEROES

The domination of English clubs in Europe continued in the early 1980s with Clough, Paisley, Dalglish and Hansen prime movers in the European Cups lifted by Nottingham Forest in 1980, Liverpool in 1981 and Aston Villa in 1982. Liverpool won again in 1984 before losing to Juventus in the tragic Heysel final in 1985, which led to English clubs been banned from Europe for five years.

Graeme Souness headed north in 1986 to manage Rangers, sparking a revolution that brought England team stalwarts Terry Butcher, Chris Woods and Gary Stevens to Glasgow.

The 1980s saw the rise of one of England's greatest ever strikers, Gary Lineker, and one of its finest ever captains, Bryan Robson, as well as the skilful management of Sir Bobby Robson for club and country. Two Welshmen also hit the headlines in the form of prolific striker Ian Rush at Liverpool and goalkeeper Neville Southall at Everton.

THE NINETIES

The 1990s saw the Sky TV revolution, the revamped European Cup (the Champions League) and the new Division One (the Premier League, better known as the 'The Premiership'), which brought glamour and money into the English game as never before. With the new riches came a host of talents from overseas.

Manchester United led the way with nine Premier League titles under the stewardship of Sir Alex Ferguson. He brought in foreign players such as the sublimely talented Eric Cantona and goalkeeper Peter Schmeichel, through British talents such as David Beckham and Ryan Giggs also excelled as Manchester United won the Champions League in 1999.

NEW MILLENNIUM

This is a decade of footballing superstars like never before with Beckham-mania reaching new heights, with other key media figures including Thierry Henry at Arsenal, Wayne Rooney at Manchester United and John Terry at Chelsea. The influx of foreign players and managers, including the highly successful Arsene Wenger at Arsenal continues.

Some commentators have suggested that this focus on individual players is having a negative impact on the national side as England joined the other Home Nations in failing to qualify for Euro 2008.

Celtic and Rangers meanwhile both qualified for the first time for the latter stages of the Champions League and shortly after the national team recorded back-to-back wins over France with Everton's James McFadden scoring the winner in Paris. Proof, perhaps, that the commentators are right, and that including more homegrown players in the domestic competitions goes hand in hand with international success.

BELOW
ARSENE WENGER, ARSENAL MANAGER. 29/04/2007

JOHN REYNOLDS, ASTON VILLA. REYNOLDS WON EIGHT CAPS FOR ENGLAND, IN WHOSE SHIRT HE IS SHOWN, AND FIVE FOR IRELAND. 1895

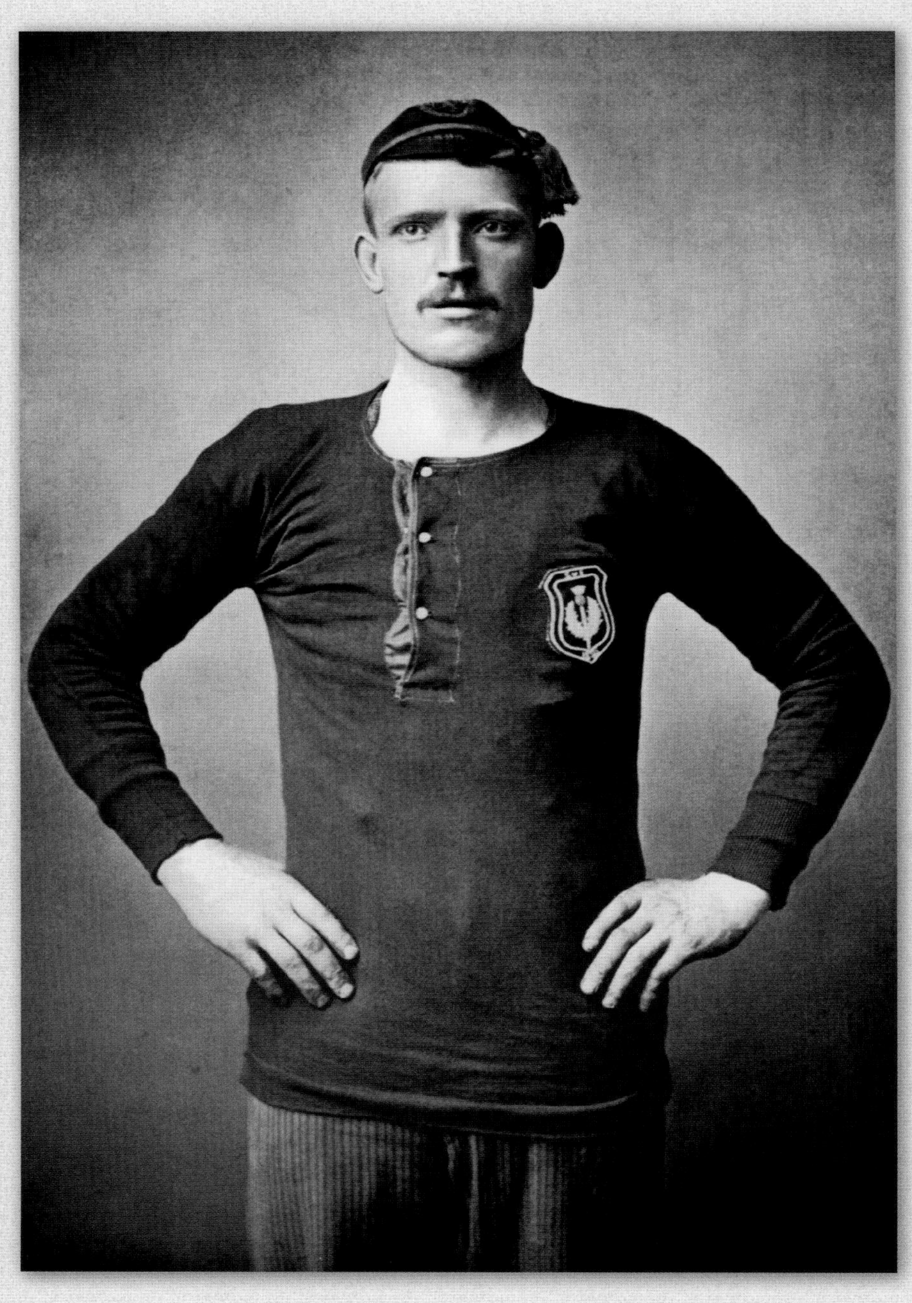

DAVID RUSSELL, HEART OF MIDLOTHIAN AND SCOTLAND. 1895

JACK HILLMAN, EVERTON GOALKEEPER. 1895

WILLIAM MOON, OLD WESTMINSTERS AND ENGLAND GOALKEEPER.1895

STEVE SMITH, ENGLAND.1895

OPPOSITE

CAESAR JENKYNS, WOOLWICH ARSENAL. 1895

G.O. SMITH, ENGLAND. 1900

STEVE BLOOMER, DERBY COUNTY AND ENGLAND. 1904

DAN CUNLIFFE, PORTSMOUTH. 1905

SAM HARDY, ASTON VILLA
GOALKEEPER. 26/10/1912

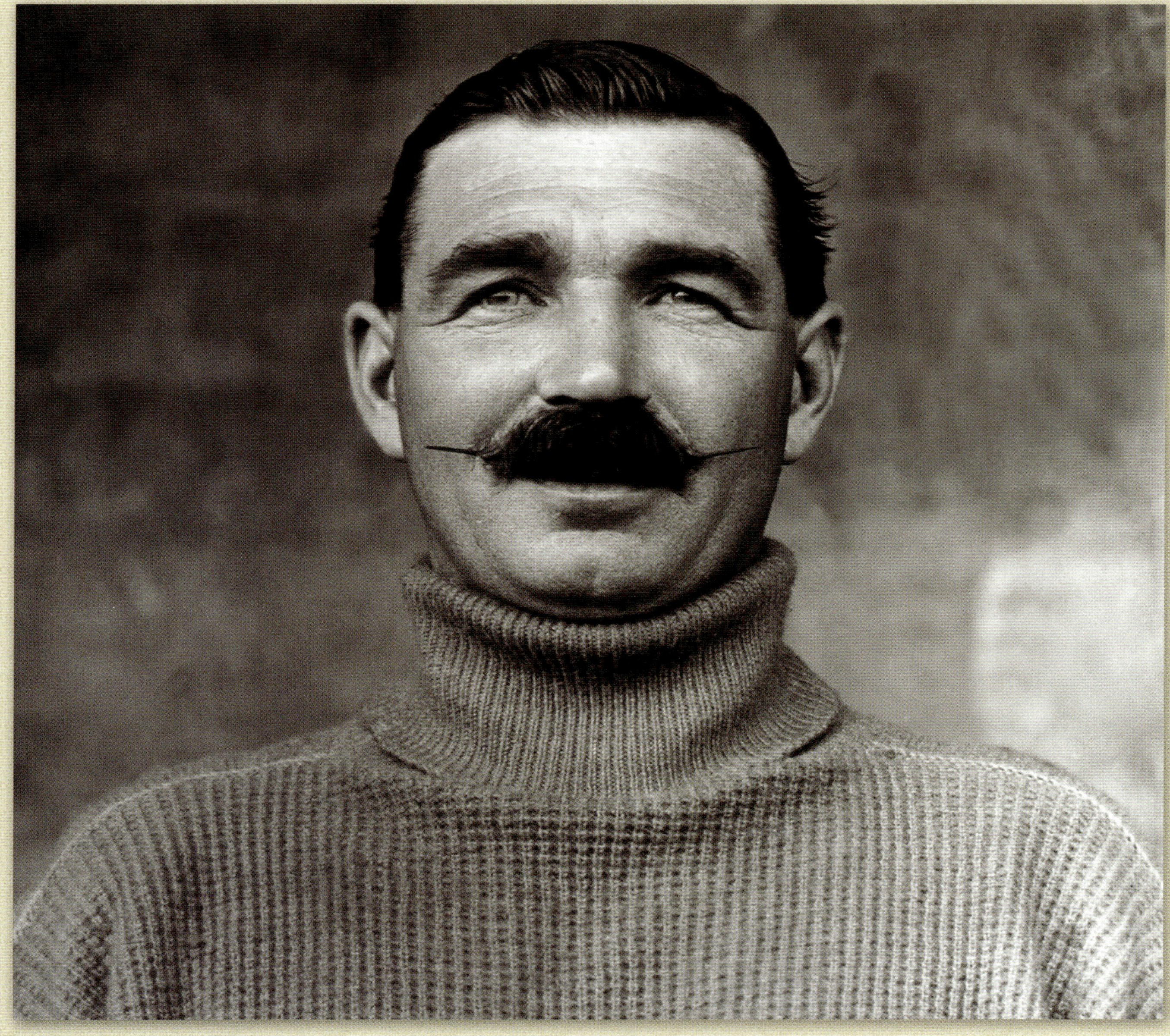

CHARLIE PAYNTER, WEST HAM UNITED TRAINER AND COACH. 1919

ARSENAL'S NEW SIGNING FRED PAGNAM AT HIGHBURY TO WATCH THE MATCH. 20/10/1919

WEST HAM UNITED CAPTAIN GEORGE KAY (L) AND BOLTON WANDERERS CAPTAIN JOE SMITH (R). 28/04/1923

WALTER ALSFORD OF TOTTENHAM HOTSPUR (R) BEING CONGRATULATED BY TEAMMATE WILLIE HALL (L) AFTER WINNING HIS FIRST ENGLAND CAP AGAINST SCOTLAND, AS THE TRAINER (WITH HAT) AND FOSTER HEADLEY (SECOND R) THE TOTTENHAM HOTSPUR CENTRE FORWARD, LOOK ON. 03/04/1925

CHARLIE BUCHAN, ARSENAL. 21/04/1927

OPPOSITE

ARTHUR GRIMSDELL, CLAPTON ORIENT MANAGER. 16/08/1929

(L-R) ALF STEWARD AND BILL DALE, MANCHESTER UNITED. 28/09/1929

BILL 'DIXIE' DEAN OF EVERTON SHOOTS FOR GOAL AT GOODISON PARK. 20/10/1930

(L-R) CHELSEA'S ALEC JACKSON AND ANDY WILSON TRAINING. 04/08/1931

ARSENAL CAPTAIN TOM PARKER LEADS HIS TEAM OUT BEFORE A MATCH. 20/02/1932

(L-R) ARSENAL TRAINER TOM WHITTAKER, STAR PLAYER ALEX JAMES AND MANAGER HERBERT CHAPMAN WATCH A MATCH FROM THE SIDELINES. 13/09/1932

OPPOSITE

SAMMY WEAVER, NEWCASTLE UNITED.

22/04/1932

HERBERT CHAPMAN, ARSENAL MANAGER. 01/08/1932

TOTTENHAM HOTSPUR GOALKEEPER JOE NICHOLLS WATCHES AS THE BALL FLIES PAST HIM ONLY TO GO WIDE OF THE GOAL. 28/08/1933

HARRY CURTIS, BRENTFORD MANAGER. 01/09/1934

WALES INTERNATIONAL WILLIAM 'WILLIE' EVANS PRACTISES SHOOTING. 01/10/1934

NOTTS COUNTY PLAYERS TRAINING AT MEADOW LANE. 18/08/1935

JACKIE CRAWFORD, QUEENS PARK RANGERS (R). 20/03/1936

LESLIE KNIGHTON, CHELSEA MANAGER. 30/04/1937

WALTER WINTERBOTTOM, MANCHESTER UNITED. 10/08/1937

LIVERPOOL GOALKEEPER ARTHUR RILEY RUSHES OUT TO CHALLENGE CHELSEA'S GEORGE MILLS. 28/08/1937

PETER DOHERTY, GUESTING FOR BRENTFORD. 07/09/1945

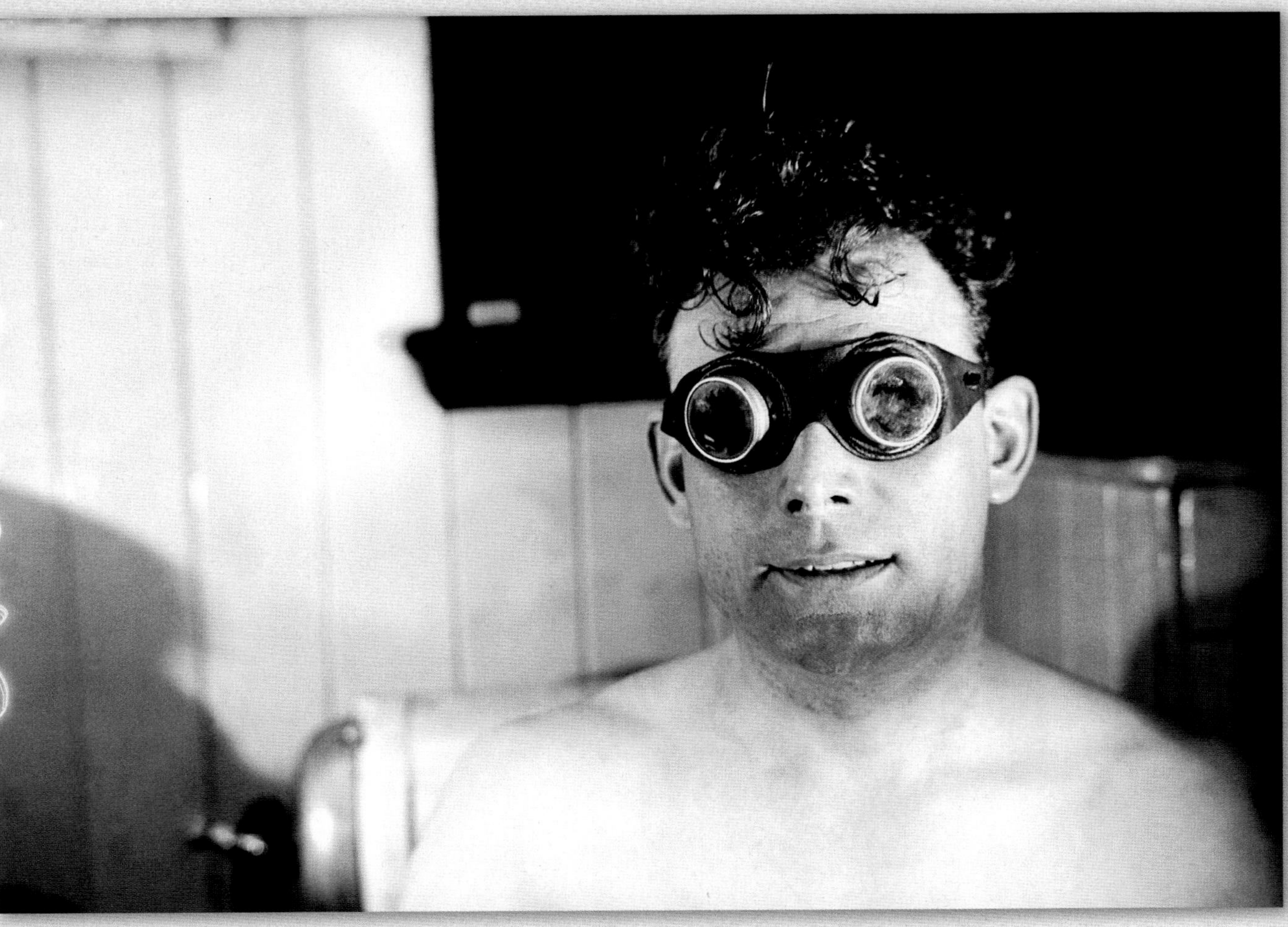

BRENTFORD'S LEN TOWNSEND PROTECTS HIS EYES WITH A PAIR OF GOGGLES WHILE TAKING IN THE RAYS FROM A SUN LAMP. 01/03/1946

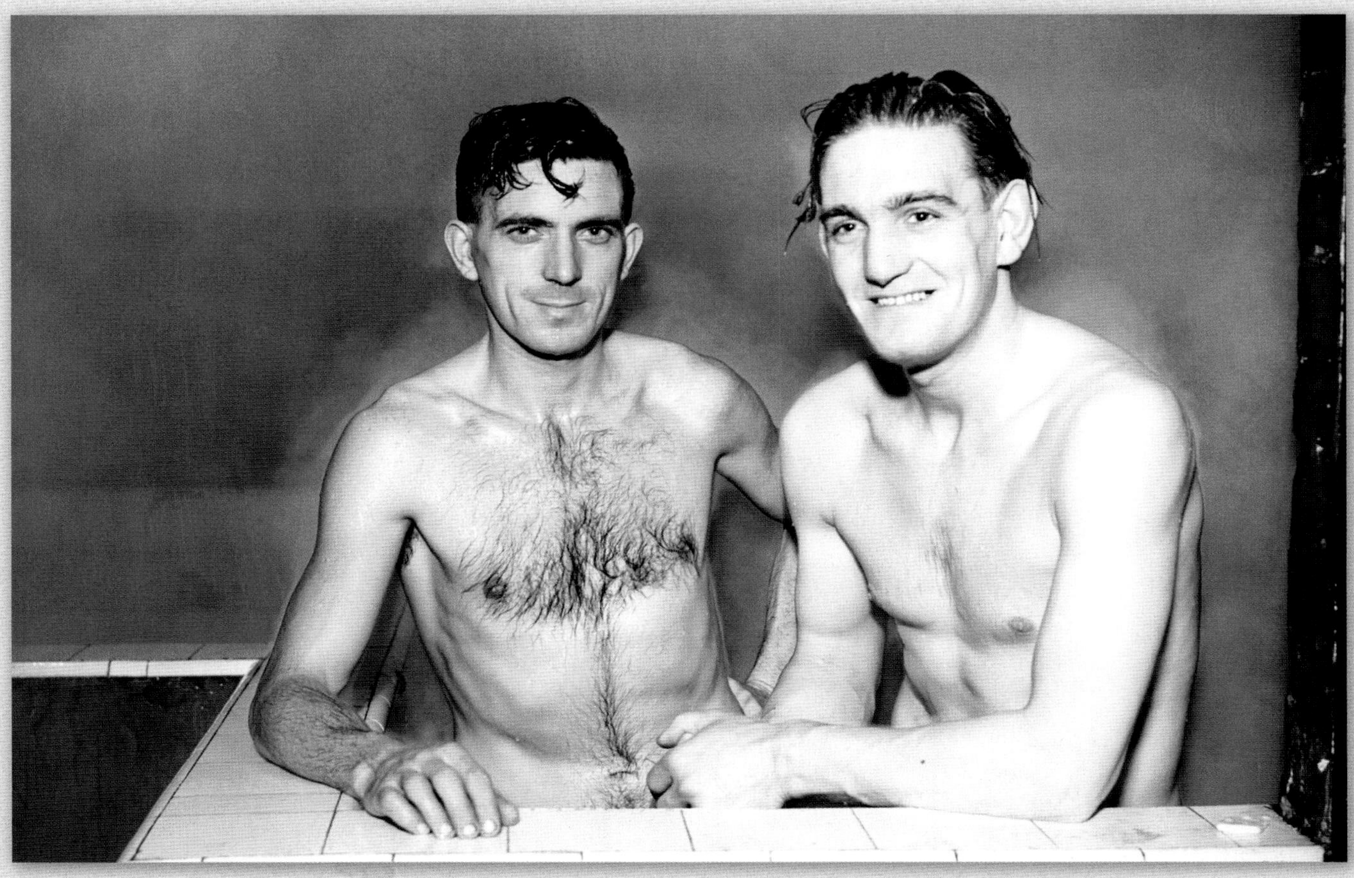

(L-R) BRENTFORD'S HARRY BAMFORD AND HARRY OLIVER ENJOY A STEAMY BRINE BATH. 01/03/1946

TOMMY LAWTON, CHELSEA. 17/08/1946

WEST BROMWICH ALBION'S BILLY ELLIOTT RUNS OUT BEFORE A MATCH. 04/01/1947

STANLEY MATTHEWS, BLACKPOOL.
28/02/1948

YEOVIL TOWN PLAYER-MANAGER ALEC STOCK AT WORK IN HIS OFFICE IMMEDIATELY AFTER TRAINING. 26/01/1949

JACKIE MILBURN, NEWCASTLE UNITED. 29/04/1949

LEN SHACKLETON, SUNDERLAND. 01/03/1950

JACKIE VERNON, WEST BROMWICH ALBION. 27/04/1950

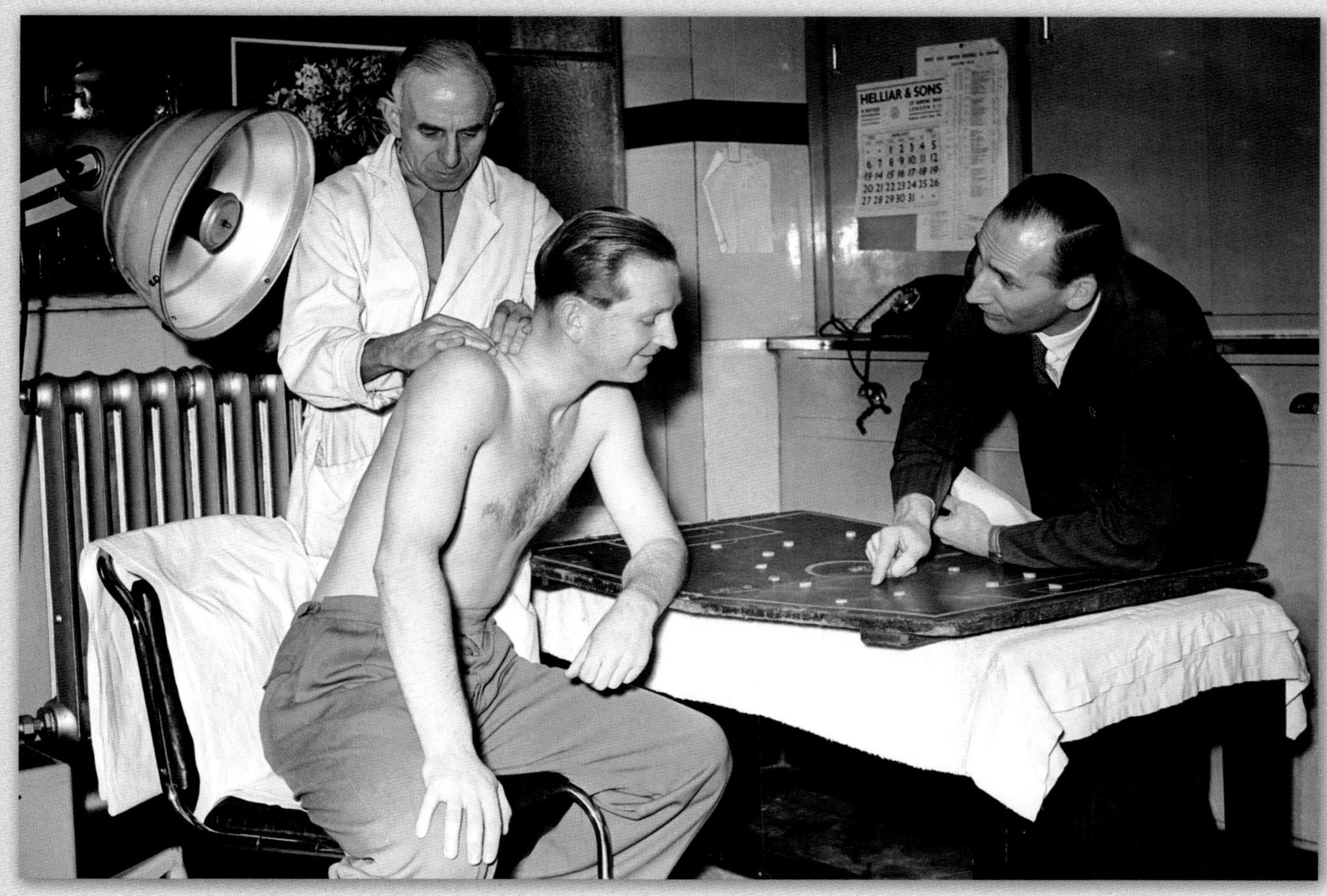

WEST HAM UNITED MANAGER TED FENTON (R) EXPLAINS A TACTICAL POINT TO HARRY KINSELL (C) WHILE KINSELL RECEIVES A MASSAGE FROM TRAINER W. MOORE (L). 04/02/1952

DUNCAN EDWARDS, ENGLAND. 31/03/1955

OPPOSITE

MANCHESTER CITY'S DAVE EWING (L) AND BILL LEIVERS (R) HELP GOALKEEPER BERT TRAUTMANN (C) OFF THE PITCH AFTER THEIR 3-1 VICTORY. TRAUTMANN HAD BROKEN HIS NECK MAKING A SAVE AT THE FEET OF BIRMINGHAM CITY'S PETER MURPHY. 05/05/1956

PRESTON NORTH END'S TOM FINNEY SPLASHES THROUGH A PUDDLE. 25/08/1956

CHARLTON ATHLETIC'S JOHNNY SUMMERS (SECOND L) BRINGS A GREAT SAVE OUT OF FULHAM GOALKEEPER TONY MACEDO (R) WITH THIS FLYING HEADER. FULHAM'S JIM LANGLEY (L) IS THE BEATEN FULL BACK. 29/01/1958

ENGLAND GOALKEEPER EDDIE HOPKINSON MAKES A FLYING SAVE. 06/05/1959

OPPOSITE

DANNY BLANCHFLOWER OF TOTTENHAM HOTSPUR CASTS A CRITICAL EYE OVER HIS BOOTS. 26/09/1958

(L-R) TERRY MEDWIN AND CLIFF JONES, TOTTENHAM HOTSPUR. 01/09/1959

BLACKBURN ROVERS AND ENGLAND CAPTAIN RONNIE CLAYTON WITH HIS WIFE VALERIE AT THEIR NEWSAGENTS SHOP IN DARWEN, LANCASHIRE. 23/10/1959

CHELSEA'S FRANK BLUNSTONE BOUNDS ACROSS THE STAMFORD BRIDGE GYM ON A POGO STICK.

28/01/1960

BLACKBURN ROVERS' DAVID WHELAN RESTS IN HOSPITAL RECOVERING FROM A BROKEN LEG. 07/05/1960

BOBBY ROBSON, WEST BROMWICH ALBION. 02/06/1960

ARSENAL GOALKEEPER JACK KELSEY STOPS AN INCREDIBLE SIX SHOTS SIMULTANEOUSLY DURING PRE-SEASON TRAINING.

16/08/1960

JOE BAKER (L) AND DENIS LAW (R) ARE ABLE TO SEE THE FUNNY SIDE OF THEIR LIFE THREATENING CAR CRASH, UPON RETURNING TO TRAINING AT TORINO. 24/04/1962

OPPOSITE

WALTER WINTERBOTTOM, ENGLAND MANAGER. 01/03/1962

TERRY PAINE, SOUTHAMPTON. 01/11/1963

BOBBY MOORE, WEST HAM UNITED. 01/02/1964

ENGLAND'S TERRY VENABLES PRACTISES HIS SPLITS IN PREPARATION FOR A GAME. 19/10/1964

CHELSEA GOALKEEPER PETER BONETTI MAKES A FLYING SAVE. 29/03/1965

(L-R) STOKE CITY'S STANLEY MATTHEWS LINES UP ALONGSIDE JIMMY GREAVES, BRYAN DOUGLAS AND ALAN GILZEAN FOR HIS TESTIMONIAL MATCH. 28/04/1965

OPPOSITE

JACK AND BOBBY CHARLTON TAKE A BREAK IN TRAINING AT STAMFORD BRIDGE, CHELSEA. 08/04/1965

PICKLES, WHO DISCOVERED THE LOST JULES RIMET TROPHY UNDER A HOLLY BUSH OUTSIDE HIS OWNER'S HOUSE, WEARING THE SILVER MEDAL THAT WAS PRESENTED TO HIM BY THE NATIONAL CANINE DEFENCE LEAGUE, WITH HIS REWARD ON A PLATE IN FRONT OF HIM. 01/04/1966

BILL SHANKLY, LIVERPOOL MANAGER. 01/08/1966

GEORGE BEST (L) AND MIKE SUMMERBEE (R) STANDING INSIDE THEIR MEN'S CLOTHING BOUTIQUE. 01/06/1967

TOTTENHAM HOTSPUR'S JIMMY GREAVES PLAYS ABOUT WITH A CAMERA. 07/08/1967

DENIS LAW, MANCHESTER UNITED. 30/09/1967

LIVERPOOL MANAGER BILL SHANKLY AT LUNCH. 1968

WEST BROMWICH ALBION MANAGER ALAN ASHMAN (L) URGES HIS TEAM ON. 18/05/1968

BRIAN CLOUGH, DERBY COUNTY MANAGER. 01/07/1969

TOMMY DOCHERTY, MANAGER OF ASTON VILLA. 01/07/1969

(L-R) PETER BONETTI, CHELSEA AND JACK CHARLTON, LEEDS UNITED. 11/04/1970

MEX
70

PELE OF BRAZIL (L) AND BOBBY CHARLTON OF ENGLAND (R) SEEN FROM THE ENGLAND BENCH. 07/06/1970

OPPOSITE

BOBBY MOORE, ENGLAND CAPTAIN. 01/05/1970

MANCHESTER UNITED'S BOBBY CHARLTON (9) AND GEORGE BEST (11) WALK BACK TO THE CENTRE CIRCLE AFTER CONCEDING A GOAL. 24/04/1971

STOKE CITY GOALKEEPER GORDON BANKS SHOWS OFF HIS GREATEST ASSETS. 30/04/1971

LIVERPOOL MANAGER BILL SHANKLY (R) WITH PLAYER KEVIN KEEGAN (L) AT ANFIELD. 24/05/1971

(R-L) WEST HAM UNITED'S GEOFF HURST, HARRY REDKNAPP, CLYDE BEST, TREVOR BROOKING, BRYAN (POP) ROBSON, RONNIE BOYCE AND JOHN AYRIS LINE UP ON THE TERRACES AT UPTON PARK. 01/10/1971

(L-R) GORDON BANKS, GEORGE EASTHAM, SCORER OF THE WINNING GOAL (BOTH STOKE CITY). STOKE CITY V CHELSEA.
04/03/1972

ENGLAND CAPTAIN BOBBY MOORE SHOWS OFF ONE OF HIS LINE OF FASHION PRODUCTS. 01/07/1972

IPSWICH TOWN MANAGER BOBBY ROBSON GIVES A GUIDED TOUR OF PORTMAN ROAD, HOME OF THE CLUB. 01/08/1972

ARSENAL PLAYERS (L-R): ALAN BALL (IN HIS WHITE BOOTS), CHARLIE GEORGE (IN HIS RED BOOTS), GEORGE ARMSTRONG, EDDIE KELLY, PETER MARINELLO AND SAMMY NELSON. 01/08/1972

ENGLAND CAPTAIN BOBBY MOORE (R) RELAXES IN THE WEMBLEY TUNNEL BEFORE A MATCH AS GOALKEEPER PETER SHILTON (L) LOOKS ON. 15/05/1973

ALEX STEPNEY, MANCHESTER UNITED GOALKEEPER. 01/08/1973

DERBY COUNTY MANAGER BRIAN CLOUGH IN THE WORLD OF SPORT STUDIOS FOR HIS DEBUT APPEARANCE AS ANALYST ON ITV'S ON THE BALL PROGRAMME. 23/08/1973

ENGLAND CAPTAIN EMLYN HUGHES (L) AND MANAGER DON REVIE (R). 28/10/1974

(L-R) ENGLAND'S EMLYN HUGHES WAITS FOR THE BRAZILIAN NATIONAL ANTHEM TO END, ALONGSIDE TEAMMATES BRIAN GREENHOFF, PHIL NEAL, TREVOR FRANCIS AND DAVE WATSON. 08/06/1977

OPPOSITE

NOTTINGHAM FOREST GOALKEEPER CHRIS WOODS ACKNOWLEDGES THE CHEERS OF THE FOREST FANS. 18/03/1978

FOREST

TOTTENHAM HOTSPUR'S OSVALDO ARDILES READS A COPY OF ONZE AT WHITE HART LANE. 01/08/1978

WEST HAM UNITED'S TREVOR BROOKING CELEBRATES SCORING A WINNING GOAL. 10/05/1980

KEVIN KEEGAN MODELS A SPORTS JACKET AND FLANNEL TROUSERS, BOTH FROM THE KEVIN KEEGAN COLLECTION AT FENTON SHOPS. 01/09/1980

ENGLAND GOALKEEPERS
RAY CLEMENCE (L) AND
PETER SHILTON (R). 15/10/1980

RON GREENWOOD, ENGLAND MANAGER. 15/10/1980

IPSWICH TOWN'S PAUL MARINER STANDS IN FRONT OF THE TEAM BUS. 06/02/1981

ARSENAL GOALKEEPER PAT JENNINGS FOOLS AROUND WITH A HOSE DURING THE CLUB'S PRE-SEASON PHOTOCALL.

25/08/1981

CHELSEA GOALKEEPER PETAR BOROTA TRIES TO PICK A PAIR OF BOOTS TO WEAR WHILE TESTING THE NEW OMNITURF SURFACE AT LOFTUS ROAD, HOME OF QUEENS PARK RANGERS. 24/06/1981

SCOTLAND'S JOE JORDAN CELEBRATES SCORING A GOAL. 09/09/1981

MANCHESTER UNITED MANAGER RON ATKINSON (L) AND CHAIRMAN MARTIN EDWARDS (R) WITH NEW SIGNING BRYAN ROBSON AT OLD TRAFFORD. 02/10/1981

DANNY MCGRAIN OF SCOTLAND TAKES A THROW IN. 10/10/1981

ENGLAND'S PAUL MARINER (R) HOOKS THE BALL BACK ACROSS THE GOAL, WATCHED BY SCOTLAND'S (L-R) PAUL HEGARTY, ALAN ROUGH, WILLIE MILLER AND DANNY MCGRAIN. 29/05/1982

GRAHAM TAYLOR, WATFORD MANAGER. 11/09/1982

LIVERPOOL'S MICHAEL ROBINSON, ALAN HANSEN AND GRAEME SOUNESS CELEBRATE. 10/04/1984

EVERTON'S ANDY GRAY CELEBRATES SCORING A GOAL. 15/05/1985

OPPOSITE

ALVIN MARTIN, WEST HAM UNITED. 10/09/1985

AVCO

SCOTLAND MANAGER JOCK STEIN (R) WITH HIS ASSISTANT ALEX FERGUSON (L). 10/09/1985

REFEREE ALAN ROBINSON IS TOLD THE WORLD'S FUNNIEST JOKE. 01/10/1985

L.F.C.
crown paints

(L-R) ENGLAND'S JOHN BARNES AND GARY LINEKER BY THE POOL AFTER TRAINING. 01/06/1986

OPPOSITE

LIVERPOOL'S IAN RUSH CELEBRATES SCORING. 10/05/1986

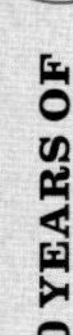

ENGLAND'S STEVE HODGE CONSIDERS WHETHER IT WOULD BE POSSIBLE TO PUNCH IN A GOAL DURING A WORLD CUP MATCH AS HE TAKES A BREAK FROM TRAINING. 01/06/1986

NOTTINGHAM FOREST LEFT BACK (AND ELECTRICIAN) STUART PEARCE DEMONSTRATES HIS PROFICIENCY AT HIS SECOND JOB. 03/09/1986

ENGLAND AND FORMER LEICESTER CITY PLAYER GARY LINEKER. 01/12/1986

DERBY GOALKEEPER BRIAN THORNTON DURING TRAINING. 29/11/1987

(L-R) MIRANDINHA AND PAUL GASCOIGNE, NEWCASTLE UNITED. 01/01/1988

VINNIE JONES, WIMBLEDON. 14/05/1988

SHEFFIELD UNITED MANAGER DAVE BASSETT (L) KISSES TONY AGANA (R) AFTER UNITED SECURED PROMOTION TO DIVISION ONE. 05/05/1990

OPPOSITE

ENGLAND'S PAUL GASCOIGNE WITH HEAD IN HANDS CRYING AFTER DEFEAT BY WEST GERMANY IN THE WORLD CUP SEMI FINAL IN TURIN. 04/07/1990

HRH DIANA, THE PRINCESS OF WALES, MEETS NOTTINGHAM FOREST'S BRIAN LAWS (L) MANAGER BRIAN CLOUGH (C) AND CAPTAIN STUART PEARCE (R) BEFORE THE FA CUP FINAL WITH TOTTENHAM HOTSPUR. 18/05/1991

LIVERPOOL GOALKEEPER BRUCE GROBBELAAR LETS OFF STEAM IN TRAINING. 27/11/1991

MANCHESTER UNITED'S ERIC CANTONA TRIES AN OVERHEAD KICK.
14/03/1993

DAVID SPEEDIE OF LEICESTER CITY (L) COMES FACE TO FACE WITH MANCHESTER UNITED GOALKEEPER PETER SCHMEICHEL (R). 27/10/1993

EVERTON'S DUNCAN FERGUSON CELEBRATES WITH A BLUE NOSE. 20/05/1995

PAUL GASCOIGNE SCORES ENGLAND'S SECOND GOAL IN SPECTACULAR FASHION AS SCOTLAND'S COLIN HENDRY (R) CAN ONLY LOOK ON. EURO 96, GROUP A MATCH, WEMBLEY STADIUM. 15/06/1996

MANCHESTER UNITED'S ERIC CANTONA CELEBRATES THE SECOND GOAL AGAINST PORTO WITH DAVID BECKHAM IN PURSUIT. UEFA CHAMPIONS LEAGUE. 05/03/1997

MANCHESTER UNITED GOALKEEPER PETER SCHMEICHEL APPLAUDS THE FANS AGAINST A BACKDROP OF RED SMOKE. 23/04/1997

ENGLAND'S BLOOD STAINED CAPTAIN PAUL INCE (C) RALLIES TONY ADAMS (R) AND SOL CAMPBELL (L). 11/10/1997

JURGEN KLINSMANN CELEBRATES SCORING ON HIS LAST APPEARANCE FOR TOTTENHAM HOTSPUR AT WHITE HART LANE.
10/05/1998

GIANFRANCO ZOLA OF CHELSEA CELEBRATES SCORING THE WINNING GOAL WITH HIS SECOND KICK OF THE GAME.
EUROPEAN CUP WINNERS' CUP FINAL AGAINST STUTTGART. 13/05/1998

BRADFORD CITY'S PETER BEAGRIE CELEBRATES AFTER SCORING FROM THE PENALTY SPOT. 14/08/1999

ALAN SHEARER, ENGLAND. 30/08/1999

(L-R) ENGLAND MANAGER SVEN GORAN ERIKSSON AND COACH STEVE MCCLAREN. 21/06/2002

CHELSEA CHAIRMAN KEN BATES.

13/09/2003

NEWCASTLE UNITED GOALKEEPER SHAY GIVEN STANDS IN THE TORRENTIAL RAIN. 01/01/2005

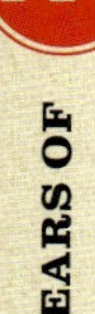

WALES MANAGER JOHN TOSHACK.

07/09/2005

NEWCASTLE UNITED'S MICHAEL OWEN (R) CELEBRATES WITH TEAMMATE ALAN SHEARER (L) AFTER SCORING THE FIRST GOAL FOR HIS CLUB, AND THE SECOND GOAL AGAINST BLACKBURN ROVERS. 18/09/2005

THIERRY HENRY, ARSENAL. 22/10/2005

OPPOSITE

MANCHESTER UNITED'S WAYNE ROONEY (R) BATTLES WITH NEWCASTLE UNITED'S CELESTINE BABAYARO (L). 12/03/2006

vodafone
northern rock

ARSENAL'S THIERRY HENRY CONTROLS THE BALL. 01/04/2006

ROBBIE SAVAGE, BLACKBURN ROVERS.
27/08/2006

CHELSEA MANAGER JOSE MOURINHO IS FILMED DURING A PRESS CONFERENCE. 24/04/2007

ENGLAND'S DAVID BECKHAM STANDS DEJECTED. 22/08/2007

Chapter Two

PLACES

THE HALLOWED TURF

The giant stadiums are atmospheric cauldrons where dreams are realised and broken.

Part of the beauty of football is that this simple game can be enjoyed anywhere in the world, from the beaches of Rio to the playing fields of Hackney. It is the giant stadiums of the UK, though, that are held dear in fans' hearts. Their stories can be as intriguing as those of any of the players and managers.

BELOW

THE PITCH AT WEMBLEY IS INVADED BY SPECTATORS AT THE FIRST FA CUP FINAL TO BE HELD THERE. 28/04/1923

WEMBLEY STADIUM

Originally designed to host the British Empire Exhibition, the first Wembley cost the princely sum of £750,000 and was built in less than a year. The first match was the 1923 FA Cup Final (a Bolton Wanderers 2-0 win over West Ham United). This became known as the 'White Horse Final' as the official 127,000 capacity was vastly exceeded by at least 100,000 fans and white police horses were needed to clear the pitch. The first international saw Scotland and England play out a 1-1 stalemate a year later. England's first defeat came at the hands of Scotland in 1928 when the legendary 'Wembley Wizards' ran out 5-1 victors.

Wembley has seen more than its fair share of pulsating FA Cup finals over the years and it was not until 1970 that it saw its first FA Cup final draw - Chelsea and Leeds were still level 2-2 after two periods of extra time failed to separate them.

The most famous game ever played on the hallowed turf, though, was the 1966 World Cup final between England and Germany when the host nation were 4-2 winners. Ironically Germany were the last team to beat England at the 'Old Wembley' before the famous 'Twin Towers' were torn down in 2003.

Today's Wembley opened in 2007. Its triple tiers and eight floors seat 90,000 and it is one of the most impressive stadiums in the world.

HAMPDEN

In Scotland the national stadium, Hampden, enjoys a similarly hallowed place in the national sporting psyche. The stadium opened in 1903 when the home side Queens Park recorded a 1-0 triumph over Celtic. The original capacity was colossal with the official crowd for the 1937 clash with England being 149,415 and it remained the largest stadium in the world until 1950 when it was finally usurped by the Maracanã in Brazil.

Hampden has been home to many tumultuous tussles including some tempestuous 'Old Firm' finals between great Glasgow rivals Rangers and Celtic. Some observers think that the best big match ever played on British soil was played here in the form of the 1960 European Cup final when 130,000 savoured Real Madrid's epic 7-3 win over Eintracht Frankfurt. The new stadium, which opened in 1999, has a seated capacity of 52,000 spread across six floors, but some diehard

ABOVE
SCOTLAND FANS WATCH A MATCH THROUGH A GAP IN THE CORNER OF HAMPDEN PARK. 25/05/1985

'Tartan Army' fans maintain that the famous 'Hampden Roar' has been dampened by the all-seated nature of the ground and its reduced capacity.

STADIUM DISASTERS

In the pre-war years, as football became more and more popular, terraces often bulged with more fans than their designated capacity. The Burnden Park disaster in 1946, which killed 33 fans, was a warning that went largely unheeded. It took until the 1980s for radical change to be kick-started after a series of tragic incidents.

In 1971 in Glasgow the Ibrox disaster led to the deaths of 66 fans as a stairway collapsed. In 1985 a fierce fire at the Valley Parade stadium in Bradford killed 56. Just a few weeks later came the Heysel disaster in Brussels, which killed 39 people and led to English clubs being banned from Europe. The decade came to a tragic end with the Hillsborough disaster in 1989 when overcrowding at the FA cup semi-final between Liverpool and Nottingham Forest left 96 fans dead.

ABOVE
A MANCHESTER UNITED FAN AT THE FRONT OF THE OLD TRAFFORD GROUND. 31/08/2004

NEW STADIUMS

The tragedies of the 1970s and 80s led to a dramatic rethink. The banning of alcohol and the introduction of all-seated stadiums were key changes. The 100,000-plus standing terrace crowds of Wembley and Hampden were firmly consigned to history. The Taylor Report, published in 1989, was instrumental in these changes. As crowd capacities were slashed many clubs struggled financially to implement the changes needed to bring their stadiums up to the new safety standards. Today, football often takes place within a huge leisure complex complete with add-ons like housing, corporate boxes, conference and incentive facilities and shops. This has become more important as clubs look to finance the huge transfer fees now involved in football.

It is Manchester United who currently boast the largest club ground in the UK with a capacity of 76,000 at Old Trafford. The 'Theatre of Dreams' is typical of the evolution of club grounds over the last 100 years. Opened in 1910, no one in the 80,000 crowd back then could have known that the small covered seated area amongst the terraces was the shape of things to come.

Old Trafford was damaged by German bombing during World War II, but it continued to be a pioneer in the post war decades. Today it is back to where it began, blazing a trail for the development of other club grounds as it continually strives to improve.

Some fans now bemoan the loss of the true 'spirit' of the game, but the 'experience' now offered by the new stadiums has helped bring in a wider spectrum of supporters with more families and children appearing. Take the 74,500 capacity Millennium Stadium in Cardiff. It may not have standing terraces, but no one doubts the immense atmosphere that it can generate. Few doubt that today's stadiums are safer than ever before.

BELOW
WEMBLEY STADIUM. 21/11/2007

GENERAL VIEW OF THE ACTION FROM THE BACK OF THE CROWD, ONE OF WHOM HAS CLIMBED A TELEGRAPH POLE FOR A BETTER VIEW. FA CUP FINAL, WOLVERHAMPTON WANDERERS V EVERTON. 25/03/1893

GENERAL VIEW OF THE ACTION FROM THE PERSPECTIVE OF ONE OF THE 45,000 CROWD WHO ASSEMBLED AT THE FALLOWFIELD GROUND, MANCHESTER. 25/03/1893

GENERAL VIEW OF THE FA CUP FINAL BETWEEN ASTON VILLA AND EVERTON, PLAYED AT THE CRYSTAL PALACE BEFORE A CROWD OF OVER 65,000. 10/04/1897

ACTION IN THE QUEENS PARK GOALMOUTH. 12/03/1901

GENERAL VIEW OF THE HUGE CROWD OF OVER 114,000 WHO ASSEMBLED AT THE CRYSTAL PALACE TO WATCH THE FA CUP FINAL BETWEEN TOTTENHAM HOTSPUR AND SHEFFIELD UNITED. 20/04/1901

SCOTLAND GOALKEEPER NED DOIG (R) MAKES AN UNORTHODOX SAVE DURING A MATCH AT SHEFFIELD. 04/04/1903

THE PAVILION IN THE CORNER OF FRATTON PARK LETS THE FANS KNOW WHERE THEY ARE. 30/09/1905

A GENERAL VIEW OF A MATCH BEING PLAYED AT CRYSTAL PALACE. 15/04/1913

ACTION IN THE HUDDERSFIELD TOWN GOALMOUTH. 24/04/1920

AERIAL VIEW OF WEMBLEY DURING THE FA CUP FINAL. 23/04/1927

THE GRAF ZEPPELIN FLIES LOW OVER WEMBLEY DURING THE FA CUP FINAL. 26/04/1930

TO TEST THE POSSIBILITIES OF FLOODLIT FOOTBALL, A TRYOUT MATCH WAS CONVENED AT THE ARSENAL PRACTICE GROUND, WHICH HAD BEEN WIRED FOR FLOODLIGHTING. 28/11/1932

ARSENAL'S TROPHIES (INCLUDING THE LEAGUE CHAMPIONSHIP TROPHY AND THE LONDON COMBINATION CUP) ARE WHEELED AROUND HIGHBURY FOR THE FANS TO VIEW AT CLOSE QUARTERS. 01/12/1934

NOTTS COUNTY PLAYERS THROW MEDICINE BALLS TO EACH OTHER DURING TRAINING. 18/08/1935

A SECTION OF THE 53,703 CROWD DURING THE TWO MINUTE SILENCE IN HONOUR OF KING GEORGE V, WHO DIED FIVE DAYS BEFORE THIS MATCH. 25/01/1936

OPPOSITE

SPECTATORS ARRIVING AT WEMBLEY STADIUM. 04/10/1941

GENERAL VIEW OF THE CROWD AT WEMBLEY STADIUM. 01/05/1943

A SECTION OF THE 85,000 CROWD SPILLS OUT OF THE PACKED STANDS ONTO THE PITCH AS SEVERAL HUNDRED DARING SOULS, DESPERATE TO SEE THE LAUDED DYNAMO MOSCOW TEAM DURING THEIR TOUR OF BRITAIN, GET AN ELEVATED, IF SOMEWHAT DANGEROUS, VIEW FROM THE ROOF OF THE STAND. CHELSEA V DYNAMO MOSCOW. 13/11/1945

A YOUNG FAN IS PASSED OVER THE HEADS OF THE CROWD TO A BETTER VIEWING POSITION AT THE FRONT OF THE TERRACE AT STAMFORD BRIDGE. 01/11/1947

SOME OF THE 98,920 FANS THAT PACKED WEMBLEY FOR THE FA CUP FINAL BETWEEN MANCHESTER UNITED AND BLACKPOOL. 24/04/1948

GENERAL VIEW OF HIGHBURY, HOME OF ARSENAL. 07/10/1949

A POLICEMAN TALKS TO A COLLEAGUE ON HIS NEW WALKIE-TALKIE TELEPHONE. 04/03/1950

CHELSEA PLAYERS WARM UP FOR A TRAINING SESSION. 21/07/1950

BLACKPOOL FANS BEFORE THE FA CUP FINAL AGAINST NEWCASTLE UNITED. 28/04/1951

THE LEAGUE CHAMPIONSHIP TROPHY, WON BY TOTTENHAM HOTSPUR THE PREVIOUS WEEK, IS CARRIED AROUND WHITE HART LANE BEFORE A MATCH. 05/05/1951

GENERAL VIEW OF A MATCH IN PROGRESS ON GOODWIN SANDS, RAMSGATE. 21/07/1952

ENTHUSIASTIC PRESTON NORTH END FANS, EQUIPPED WITH BELLS AND RATTLES, WAIT FOR THE KICK OFF AT WEMBLEY.
01/05/1954

ARSENAL'S BOOT-ROOM BOY DANNY CRIPPS EXAMINES TOMMY LAWTON'S BOOTS. 03/02/1955

(L-R) JIM FOTHERINGHAM, DAVE BOWEN AND DEREK TAPSCOTT WORKING OUT IN ARSENAL'S HIGHBURY GYMNASIUM.
03/02/1955

THE SCENE DURING THE FIRST GAME AT WEMBLEY TO BE PLAYED UNDER FLOODLIGHTS. 26/10/1955

BOURNEMOUTH AND BOSCOMBE ATHLETIC FANS SHOW THEIR SUPPORT BEFORE A MATCH. 02/03/1957

THE CROWD AT ST JAMES'S PARK, NEWCASTLE. 01/01/1960

ARSENAL'S NEW SIGNING GEORGE EASTHAM ADMIRES HIGHBURY'S MARBLE ENTRANCE HALL. 18/11/1960

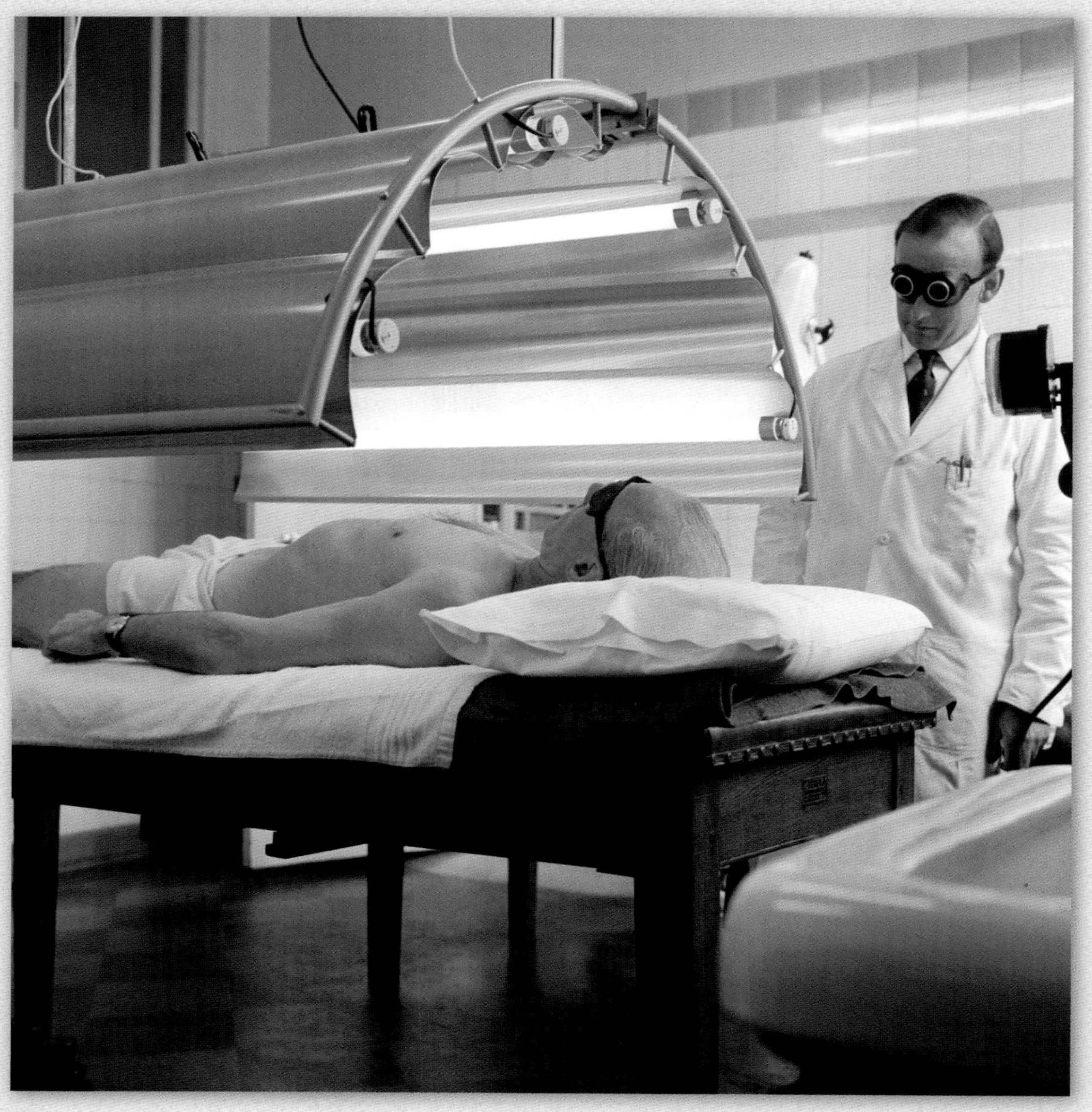

ARSENAL PHYSIOTHERAPIST BERTIE MEE USING REVOLUTIONARY NEW TECHNIQUES TO TREAT AN INJURED PATIENT.
14/04/1961

GENERAL VIEW OF THE WHITE CITY, HOME OF QUEENS PARK RANGERS, DURING A MATCH. 06/10/1962

BRIGHTON AND HOVE ALBION FANS GET A SLIGHTLY ELEVATED VIEW OF A MATCH BY STANDING ON SLABS OF FROZEN SNOW ON THE TERRACES. 12/01/1963

WALTHAMSTOW AVENUE GOALKEEPER G. MCGUIRE KEEPS WARM BY THRUSTING HIS HANDS DOWN HIS TRACKSUIT TROUSERS. 12/01/1963

ARSENAL MANAGER BILLY WRIGHT (CROUCHED) INSPECTS THE ELECTRIC CABLES WHICH RUN UNDERNEATH THE PITCH, WATCHED BY SEVERAL OF HIS PLAYERS. 24/04/1964

THE POLICE MOVE IN TO STOP TROUBLE ON LIVERPOOL'S KOP. 07/11/1966

A WINTER'S DAY AT MOLYNEUX, HOME OF WOLVERHAMPTON WANDERERS. 03/12/1966

PASTING UP A POSTER ADVERTISING THE FORTHCOMING FIXTURES TAKING PLACE AT ST ANDREWS. 09/02/1968

OPPOSITE

(L-R) NEW CHELSEA MANAGER DAVE SEXTON STANDS ON THE STAMFORD BRIDGE TERRACES WITH CHAIRMAN CHARLES PRATT. 23/10/1967

THE EVACUATED CROWD WATCHES FROM THE PITCH AS THE MAIN STAND OF NOTTINGHAM FOREST'S CITY GROUND BURNS DOWN. 24/08/1968

A WEST BROMWICH ALBION FAN ENCOURAGES HIS FELLOW SUPPORTERS TO SING UP IN SUPPORT OF THEIR TEAM.

29/03/1969

PEEL PARK, HOME OF FORMER FOOTBALL LEAGUE CLUB ACCRINGTON STANLEY. 01/06/1969

A POLICEMAN ENCOURAGES A YOUNG BLACKPOOL FAN BACK INTO THE CROWD AS A GOAL CAUSES MASS DELIRIUM AMONGST THE HOME SUPPORTERS. 22/08/1970

THE MAIN ENTRANCE TO THE VALLEY, HOME OF CHARLTON ATHLETIC. 21/11/1970

ARSENAL PLAYERS FACE THE CAMERAS AS A PRELUDE TO THE 1971-72 SOCCER SEASON. 13/08/1971

TOTTENHAM HOTSPUR
FOOTBALL CLUB

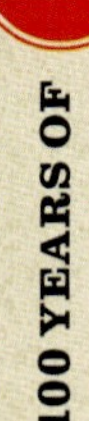

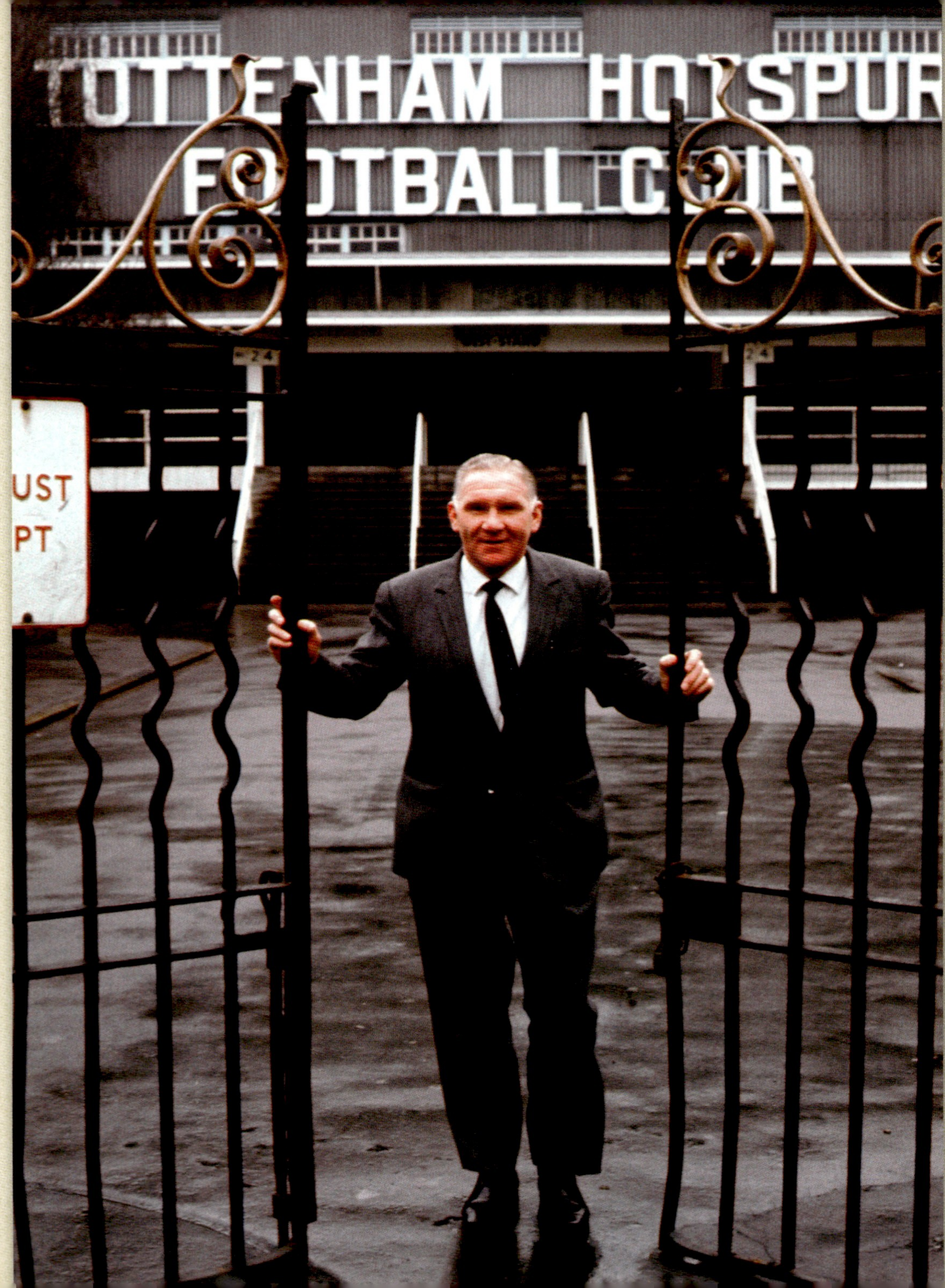

THE MAIN ENTRANCE TO THE OLD SHOW GROUND, HOME OF SCUNTHORPE UNITED. 01/10/1975

OPPOSITE

BILL NICHOLSON, TOTTENHAM HOTSPUR. 01/01/1974

PARKHEAD, HOME OF CELTIC FC. 01/01/1978

ASTON VILLA FANS CELEBRATE WINNING THE LEAGUE CHAMPIONSHIP, DESPITE A 2-0 DEFEAT AGAINST ARSENAL.

02/05/1981

FANS AT THE VETCH, HOME OF SWANSEA CITY. 29/08/1981

HALF EMPTY TERRACES AT THE CLOCK END OF HIGHBURY, HOME OF ARSENAL. 30/10/1982

WORKMEN BEGIN LAYING THE NEW GRASS PITCH AT QUEENS PARK RANGERS' LOFTUS ROAD AFTER THE ARTIFICIAL PITCH WAS TORN UP. 10/06/1988

A NOTTINGHAM FOREST FAN CLIMBS TO THE TOP OF A FLOODLIGHT TO GET THE BEST VIEW IN THE GROUND. 30/04/1994

FANS IN THE STAND PRIOR TO THE MATCH BEING ABANDONED. FA CUP FIFTH ROUND, NOTTINGHAM FOREST V TOTTENHAM HOTSPUR. 19/02/1996

THE ST GEORGE'S CROSS FLAG FLIES AGAINST A VIVID SUNSET AT WEMBLEY STADIUM. 24/04/1996

VIEW OF THE ACTION FROM GROUND LEVEL DURING STOKE CITY'S LAST MATCH AT THE VICTORIA GROUND. 04/05/1997

THE SHANKLY GATES AT ANFIELD, HOME OF LIVERPOOL. 10/07/1997

Chapter Three

MOMENTS

HIGHS & LOWS

It is meant to be the taking part and not the winning that counts, but few football fans would agree.

For the serious football supporter, winning counts for everything and the disasters on the pitch are as painfully felt as the triumphs are rapturously celebrated.

UPSETS

Every fan has his or her own personal upset, whether it is David Beckham's sending off and the subsequent defeat to Argentina during the World Cup in 1998, Scotland losing to a soft late goal to Brazil in the opening game of the same tournament, or Wales narrowly losing out in the race to qualify for the 1986 World Cup.

England may have famously beaten Germany in 1966, but it took until Euro 2000 for them to repeat this in a competitive match. In between there were painful defeats for England at both the 1970 and 1990 World Cup finals and at Wembley during Euro 96.

Scotland qualified for five World Cups in a row from 1974 through to 1990, but failed to make it to the group stages in any of them. Bad defeats and poor draws are ingrained on the

LEFT

ENGLAND'S STEVEN GERRARD SITS DEJECTED AFTER THE FINAL WHISTLE, AS CROATIA PLAYERS CELEBRATE VICTORY IN THE EURO 2008 QUALIFYING MATCH. DEFEAT MEANT ENGLAND FAILED TO QUALIFY. 21/11/2007

THOUSANDS OF FANS, FRIENDS AND FAMILY GATHERING AT ANFIELD STADIUM AROUND A PITCH FULL OF FLOWERS FOR THE CEREMONY OF REMEMBRANCE FOR ALL THOSE THAT DIED IN THE TRAGIC HILLSBOROUGH DISASTER. 22/04/1989

fans' memories along with the painful knowledge that they were only denied qualification on goal difference in three of the five tournaments.

DEFEATS

Perhaps the ultimate defeat is vying for the league title all season long, only to fall on the final day of the season. This bitter fate has befallen a number of teams, with Liverpool memorably losing the title to the last kick of the season when Michael Thomas scored Arsenal's decisive second goal at Anfield in 1989. In Scotland, Celtic suffered the same fate twice in three years; in 2003, when Rangers pipped Celtic by a single goal, and in 2005 two very late goals from Motherwell striker Scott McDonald meant that Rangers won the title and dashed Celtic's hopes.

TRAGEDIES

A string of tragedies have afflicted the game over the last century, bringing terrible losses to families and tarnishing football's good name. The stadium disasters from the 1970s through to the late 1980s still haunt the game today.

One of British football's most tragic days was 6 February 1958, when many of the 'Busby Babes' were killed in the Munich Air Disaster. These darker moments are never forgotten by fans with commemorations of their anniversaries still an essential and deeply ingrained part of club culture today.

LEFT

(L-R) BOLTON WANDERERS' JIMMY SEDDON AND JIM MCCLELLAND DISPLAY THE FA CUP. 27/04/1929

BELOW

ENGLAND'S PAUL GASCOIGNE (ON FLOOR) WITH TEDDY SHERINGHAM (L) AFTER SCORING. 15/06/1996

TRIUMPHS

England's 1966 World Cup win still delights England fans as does Gascoigne's wonder strike to finish off Scotland at Euro 96. For Scottish fans, there is the 3-2 win in 1967 over England and Archie Gemmill's famous dribble and wonder goal in the dramatic 3-2 win over Holland in the 1978 World Cup. Wales fans can think fondly of the 1958 World Cup and their unbeaten run to the knockout stages.

Recent club triumphs that stand out in England include Manchester United's stunning late comeback in the Champions League final against Bayern Munich in 1999, when they fought back from 1-0 down in the dying seconds to score twice and lift the trophy for the first time since 1968.

Then there was Liverpool's dramatic comeback in the Champions League final of 2005. They were down 3-0 to AC Milan at half-time, but a trio of goals in a six minute spell turned the game on its head and Liverpool ran out winners after a nailbiting penalty shoot-out.

On the domestic front winning the league is unquestionably the big one, as it tends to reward the best performance across the whole season. The honour of winning the old Division One/new Premier League has gone to a total of 23 clubs since the first championship title was awarded to Preston North End in 1889.

The English FA Cup is the perfect forum for triumphs when so much can change in an instant. Great minnow performances include Brighton & Hove Albion making it to the FA Cup final in 1983 and coming within a whisker of upstaging Manchester United before losing out in a replay. Wimbledon went one better in 1988, beating Liverpool 1-0.

North of the border, both Celtic and Rangers boast a long list of domestic triumphs. Celtic between 1966 and 1974 won a staggering nine titles in a row, while Rangers equalled the feat between 1989 and 1997. A string of other Scottish clubs, of course, have also won the top division and there was also the Cup Winners' Cup final 2-1 triumph over Real Madrid for Alex Ferguson's Aberdeen in 1983 and Dundee United's impressive runs to the European Cup semi-final in 1984 and the UEFA Cup final in 1987.

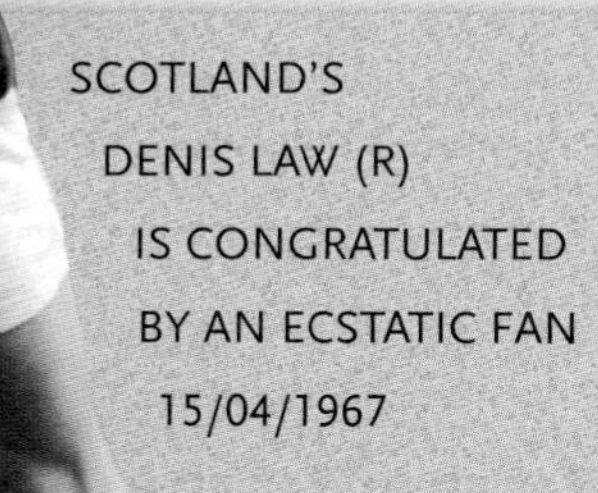

SCOTLAND'S DENIS LAW (R) IS CONGRATULATED BY AN ECSTATIC FAN 15/04/1967

ASTON VILLA CAPTAIN HOWARD SPENCER WITH THE FA CUP AFTER THE PRESENTATION, WHICH WAS MADE BY LORD KINNAIRD (C, WITH BEARD). VILLA HAD BEATEN NEWCASTLE UNITED IN THE FINAL. 15/04/1905

ARSENAL CAPTAIN TOM PARKER (THIRD L) KEEPS A TIGHT GRIP ON THE FA CUP AS HE AND HIS TEAMMATES PARADE THE TROPHY AROUND WEMBLEY: (L-R) CLIFF BASTIN, CHARLIE PREEDY, TOM PARKER, BILL SEEDON, JOE HULME, JACK LAMBERT. 26/04/1930

ARSENAL TEAM GROUP WITH TROPHIES (L-R) THE NORTHAMPTON HOSPITAL SHIELD, THE EVENING NEWS CRICKET CUP, THE LEAGUE CHAMPIONSHIP TROPHY, THE SHERIFF OF LONDON'S SHIELD, THE CHARITY SHIELD AND THE COMBINATION CUP. 23/04/1931

EVERTON'S BILL 'DIXIE' DEAN HOLDS UP THE FA CUP AS THE TEAM EMERGE ONTO LIME STREET, LIVERPOOL. 01/05/1933

THE 3RD COLDSTREAM GUARDS CHAIR THEIR CAPTAIN, HOLDING THE CUP, AS THEY CELEBRATE THEIR 2-1 VICTORY OVER THE GUARDS DEPOT IN THE HOUSEHOLD BRIGADE SENIOR CUP FINAL. 02/04/1935

ARSENAL CAPTAIN ALEX JAMES SHOWS OFF THE FA CUP AS HE IS HELD UP BY HIS VICTORIOUS TEAMMATES. 25/04/1936

THE WINNING CAPTAIN, PRESTON NORTH END'S TOM SMITH, SHOWS OFF THE FA CUP AS HE IS CHAIRED AROUND THE PITCH. 30/04/1938

PORTSMOUTH CAPTAIN JIMMY GUTHRIE HOLDS THE FA CUP ALOFT AS HE IS CHAIRED BY HIS TEAMMATES. 29/04/1939

CHARLTON ATHLETIC'S BERT JOHNSON (R) LOOKS UP AT CAPTAIN DON WELSH (C) AS HE SHOWS OFF THE FA CUP WHILST BEING CARRIED SHOULDER HIGH BY TRIUMPHANT TEAMMATES JACK SHREEVE (SECOND L) AND PETER CROKER (SECOND R). 26/04/1947

ARSENAL CAPTAIN JOE MERCER (C) CLINGS ON TO THE FA CUP AS HE IS CARRIED SHOULDER HIGH BY JUBILANT TEAMMATES. 29/04/1950

BLACKPOOL CAPTAIN HARRY JOHNSTON (TOP, L) HOLDS THE FA CUP ALOFT AFTER HIS TEAM CAME BACK FROM 3-1 DOWN TO WIN 4-3 AGAINST BOLTON WANDERERS, THANKS TO INSPIRED PERFORMANCES FROM STANLEY MATTHEWS (TOP, R), HAT TRICK HERO STAN MORTENSEN (R) AND WINNING GOALSCORER BILL PERRY (THIRD L). 02/05/1953

MANCHESTER CITY CAPTAIN ROY PAUL SHOWS OFF THE FA CUP AFTER HIS TEAM'S 3-1 VICTORY OVER BIRMINGHAM CITY. HE IS SUPPORTED BY TEAMMATES (L-R) BOBBY JOHNSTONE, DAVE EWING, DON REVIE AND KEN BARNES. 05/05/1956

BOLTON WANDERERS CAPTAIN AND CENTRE-FORWARD NAT LOFTHOUSE, WHO SCORED BOTH HIS TEAM'S GOALS, IS GIVEN A DRINK FROM THE FA CUP BY MANAGER BILL RIDDING IN THE DRESSING ROOM AT WEMBLEY AFTER BOLTON HAD BEATEN MANCHESTER UNITED 2-0 IN THE FINAL. 03/05/1958

TOTTENHAM HOTSPUR CAPTAIN DANNY BLANCHFLOWER POSES WITH THE FA CUP. 03/08/1962

IN THE FA CUP FINAL, LEICESTER CITY GOALKEEPER GORDON BANKS LOOKS DOWN DEJECTEDLY AS MANCHESTER UNITED'S DAVID HERD (L) CELEBRATES SCORING WITH TEAMMATES DENIS LAW (SECOND L), JOHNNY GILES (THIRD L) AND BOBBY CHARLTON (R). 25/05/1963

OPPOSITE

MANCHESTER UNITED'S NOEL CANTWELL (C) THROWS THE FA CUP INTO THE AIR, WATCHED BY ASTONISHED TEAMMATES (L-R) TONY DUNNE, BOBBY CHARLTON, PAT CRERAND, ALBERT QUIXALL AND DAVID HERD. 25/05/1963

OXFORD UNITED CAPTAIN RON ATKINSON (C) IS CARRIED OFF BY EUPHORIC FANS AFTER HIS TEAM BEAT FIRST DIVISION BLACKBURN ROVERS 3-1 IN THE FIFTH ROUND OF THE FA CUP. 15/02/1964

WEST HAM UNITED CELEBRATE WITH THE EUROPEAN CUP WINNERS' CUP AFTER THEIR 2-0 WIN OVER TSV 1860 MUNICH. (BACK ROW, L-R) ALAN SEALEY, MARTIN PETERS, BOBBY MOORE (WITH CUP), GEOFF HURST, JOHN SISSONS, KEN BROWN; (FRONT ROW, L-R) BRIAN DEAR, RONNIE BOYCE, JACK BURKETT. 19/05/1965

ENGLAND MANAGER ALF RAMSEY (SECOND R) EXPLAINS HIS IDEAS TO ENGLAND PLAYERS (L-R) GORDON BANKS, GEORGE COHEN, JACK CHARLTON, PETER THOMPSON, JIMMY GREAVES, BOBBY TAMBLING, BOBBY CHARLTON, AS COACH HAROLD SHEPHERDSON (R) LOOKS ON. 01/06/1966

ENGLAND CAPTAIN BOBBY MOORE IS PRESENTED WITH THE JULES RIMET TROPHY BY HER MAJESTY THE QUEEN AS TEAMMATE GEOFF HURST (R) LOOKS ON IN AWE. 30/07/1966

ENGLAND'S MARTIN PETERS, GEORGE COHEN, JACK CHARLTON, BOBBY MOORE, RAY WILSON AND BOBBY CHARLTON PARADE THE JULES RIMET TROPHY AROUND WEMBLEY FOLLOWING THEIR 4-2 VICTORY OVER WEST GERMANY. 30/07/1966

LIVERPOOL MANAGER BILL SHANKLY CROUCHES BY THE TROPHIES THAT HIS TEAM WON THE PREVIOUS SEASON, INCLUDING THE LEAGUE CHAMPIONSHIP TROPHY AND THE FA CHARITY SHIELD. 15/08/1966

ENGLAND TEAM GROUP. BACK ROW (L-R) HAROLD SHEPHERDSON, NOBBY STILES, ROGER HUNT, GORDON BANKS, JACK CHARLTON, GEORGE COHEN, RAY WILSON, MANAGER SIR ALF RAMSEY. FRONT ROW (L-R) MARTIN PETERS, GEOFF HURST, BOBBY MOORE, ALAN BALL, BOBBY CHARLTON. 02/11/1966

SCOTLAND'S DENIS LAW (R) IS CONGRATULATED BY AN ECSTATIC FAN AFTER HIS TEAM'S 3-2 VICTORY OVER ENGLAND IN THE EUROPEAN CHAMPIONSHIP QUALIFIER. 15/04/1967

LEEDS UNITED CAPTAIN BILLY BREMNER HOLDS THE LEAGUE CUP ALOFT AS HIS TEAMMATES CARRY HIM ON THEIR SHOULDERS. 02/03/1968

WEST BROMWICH ALBION CAPTAIN GRAHAM WILLIAMS CELEBRATES WITH THE FA CUP AFTER WEST BROM BEAT EVERTON IN THE FINAL. 18/05/1968

NOBBY STILES WITH THE EUROPEAN CUP AFTER MANCHESTER UNITED BEAT BENFICA 4-1 IN THE FINAL. (L-R) BRIAN KIDD, TONY DUNN, NOBBY STILES, ALEX STEPNEY AND PAT CRERAND. 29/05/1968

MANCHESTER UNITED'S GEORGE BEST (C) SHOWS OFF THE 1968 EUROPEAN FOOTBALLER OF THE YEAR AWARD, AS TEAMMATES BOBBY CHARLTON (SECOND L, 1966 WINNER) AND DENIS LAW (R, 1964 WINNER), AND MANAGER MATT BUSBY (SECOND R) LOOK ON. 19/04/1969

MANCHESTER CITY CAPTAIN TONY BOOK IS CARRIED ON MIKE DOYLE'S SHOULDERS AS L-R, GLYN PARDOE, FRANCIS LEE, HARRY DOWD AND COLIN BELL CELEBRATE WINNING THE FA CUP. 26/04/1969

EVERTON'S ALAN BALL MARCHES BACK TO THE HOME DRESSING ROOM WITH THE FOOTBALL LEAGUE CHAMPIONSHIP TROPHY UNDER HIS ARM AFTER HIS TEAM'S 2-0 WIN OVER WEST BROMWICH ALBION WRAPPED UP THE TITLE. 01/04/1970

ARSENAL GOALKEEPER BOB WILSON LEAPS FOR JOY AS THE GUNNERS' THIRD GOAL ENTERS THE ANDERLECHT NET TO GIVE THE LONDONERS A 4-3 AGGREGATE VICTORY IN THE EUROPEAN FAIRS CUP FINAL AT HIGHBURY. 28/04/1970

CHELSEA'S JOHN HOLLINS (SECOND L) AND PETER OSGOOD (R) CELEBRATE WITH THE FA CUP IN THE PLUNGE BATH, ALONGSIDE TEAMMATES TOMMY BALDWIN (L), PETER BONETTI (C) AND DAVID WEBB (SECOND R). 29/04/1970

MANCHESTER CITY CAPTAIN TONY BOOK (C) IS PRESENTED WITH THE EUROPEAN CUP WINNERS' CUP AFTER HIS TEAM'S 2-1 VICTORY OVER GORNIK ZABRZE. 29/04/1970

ARSENAL CAPTAIN FRANK MCLINTOCK (R) LETS FANS IN UPPER STREET, ISLINGTON, HAVE A TOUCH OF THE FA CUP DURING THE TEAM'S CELEBRATORY TOUR OF NORTH LONDON. 09/05/1971

HEREFORD UNITED PLAYERS ARE MOBBED BY THE JUBILANT HOME CROWD AFTER THEIR 2-1 WIN OVER NEWCASTLE UNITED IN THE THIRD ROUND FA CUP REPLAY. 05/02/1972

STOKE CITY WITH THE LEAGUE CUP. 01/04/1972

NORWICH CITY CELEBRATE WINNING THE SECOND DIVISION CHAMPIONSHIP IN THE DRESSING ROOM: (L-R) GRAHAM PADDON, TRAINER, DOUG LIVERMORE, KEVIN KEELAN, TERRY ANDERSON, DUNCAN FORBES, MANAGER RON SAUNDERS, TREVOR HOWARD. 29/04/1972

OPPOSITE

LEEDS UNITED'S ALLAN CLARKE CELEBRATES WITH THE TOP OF THE FA CUP, AND HIS CHARLES BUCHAN'S FOOTBALL MONTHLY MAN OF THE MATCH AWARD. 06/05/1972

surance
ENTENARY
CUP FINAL
1972
En

LIVERPOOL MANAGER BILL SHANKLY TAKES AN ADMIRING LOOK AT THE FOOTBALL LEAGUE CHAMPIONSHIP TROPHY. 27/04/1973

ENGLAND'S PETER SHILTON (L) AND ROY MCFARLAND (R) TRUDGE OFF THE FIELD AFTER THE TEAM'S FAILURE TO QUALIFY FOR THE 1974 WORLD CUP FINALS IN WEST GERMANY. 17/10/1973

(L-R) ASTON VILLA GOALKEEPER JOHN BURRIDGE AND HAT TRICK HERO BRIAN LITTLE CELEBRATE REACHING WEMBLEY AFTER THEIR TEAM'S 3-0 VICTORY OVER QPR. 22/02/1977

(L-R) LIVERPOOL'S PHIL NEAL, EMLYN HUGHES AND JIMMY CASE SHOW THE EUROPEAN CUP TO THEIR JUBILANT FANS.
25/05/1977

JUBILANT SCOTLAND FANS DEMOLISH THE WEMBLEY GOALPOSTS AFTER SEEING THEIR TEAM WIN 2-1 AGAINST ENGLAND.

04/06/1977

IPSWICH TOWN'S PAUL COOPER (C) AND MICK MILLS (R) CELEBRATE WITH THE FA CUP, AS TEAMMATE GEORGE BURLEY (L) WAVES TO THE FANS. 06/05/1978

LIVERPOOL'S KENNY DALGLISH (C) IS CONGRATULATED BY HIS TEAMMATES AFTER SCORING THE WINNING GOAL AGAINST CLUB BRUGGE IN THE EUROPEAN CUP FINAL. 10/05/1978

LIVERPOOL'S KENNY DALGLISH WAKES UP WITH THE EUROPEAN CUP AFTER SCORING THE WINNING GOAL IN THE PREVIOUS NIGHT'S FINAL. 11/05/1978

NOTTINGHAM FOREST'S WINNING GOALSCORER TREVOR FRANCIS CELEBRATES WITH THE EUROPEAN CUP. 30/05/1979

NOTTINGHAM FOREST'S LARRY LLOYD CELEBRATES AFTER FOREST WON THEIR SECOND SUCCESSIVE EUROPEAN CUP.
28/05/1980

(L-R) IPSWICH TOWN'S ALAN BRAZIL AND ARNOLD MUHREN CELEBRATE WINNING THE FIRST LEG OF THE UEFA CUP FINAL AGAINST AZ67 ALKMAAR 3-0, AS TEAMMATES MICK MILLS AND PAUL MARINER HUG JUBILANTLY. 06/05/1981

LIVERPOOL'S WINNING GOALSCORER ALAN KENNEDY CELEBRATES WITH THE EUROPEAN CUP. 27/05/1981

ASTON VILLA'S PETER WITHE (L) SCORES THE WINNING GOAL AGAINST BAYERN MUNICH IN THE EUROPEAN CUP FINAL.
26/05/1982

ENGLAND'S BRYAN ROBSON (R) CELEBRATES WITH TEAMMATE TERRY BUTCHER (C) AFTER SCORING THE FASTEST GOAL IN WORLD CUP HISTORY - JUST 27 SECONDS AFTER KICK OFF. THE MATCH WAS AGAINST FRANCE. 16/06/1982

LIVERPOOL MANAGER BOB PAISLEY SHOWS OFF THE LEAGUE CHAMPIONSHIP TROPHY TO THE FANS. 07/05/1983

ABERDEEN'S JOHN HEWITT SCORES THE WINNING GOAL OF THE EUROPEAN CUP WINNERS' CUP FINAL IN EXTRA TIME AGAINST REAL MADRID. 11/05/1983

ABERDEEN'S MANAGER ALEX FERGUSON (L) CELEBRATES VICTORY OVER REAL MADRID IN THE EUROPEAN CUP WINNERS' CUP FINAL WITH COACH ARCHIE KNOX (R). 11/05/1983

BOURNEMOUTH TRAINER JOHN KIRK (C, WEARING CAP) JOINS THE JUBILANT PLAYERS IN THE BATH CELEBRATING AN FA CUP THIRD ROUND VICTORY OVER MANCHESTER UNITED. ASSISTANT MANAGER STUART MORGAN (R) SUPPLIES THE CHAMPAGNE. 07/01/1984

LIVERPOOL'S BRUCE GROBBELAAR AND MICHAEL ROBINSON WITH THE EUROPEAN CUP AFTER BEATING ROMA IN THE FINAL.

30/05/1984

ARGENTINA'S DIEGO MARADONA (R) FLIES PAST ENGLAND GOALKEEPER PETER SHILTON (L) AFTER USING HIS FIST TO SCORE THE INFAMOUS 'HAND OF GOD' GOAL, IN THE WORLD CUP QUARTER FINAL MATCH. 22/06/1986

ENGLAND COACH DON HOWE (L) AND PHYSIOTHERAPIST NORMAN MEDHURST (R) CONSOLE MANAGER BOBBY ROBSON (C) AS CHRIS WADDLE MISSES A VITAL PENALTY IN THE SHOOT OUT AGAINST WEST GERMANY IN THE WORLD CUP SEMI FINAL. ENGLAND LOST IN THE PENALTY SHOOT OUT. 04/07/1990

ENGLAND'S STUART PEARCE WALKS AWAY AFTER MISSING A PENALTY IN THE SHOOT OUT AGAINST WEST GERMANY IN THE WORLD CUP SEMI FINAL. 04/07/1990

ENGLAND MANAGER GRAHAM TAYLOR MUTTERS THE IMMORTAL WORDS "YOUR MATE'S JUST COST ME MY JOB" TO THE LINESMAN. WORLD CUP QUALIFIER V HOLLAND.13/10/1993

OPPOSITE

LEEDS UNITED'S ERIC CANTONA LIFTS THE LEAGUE CHAMPIONSHIP TROPHY.
02/05/1992

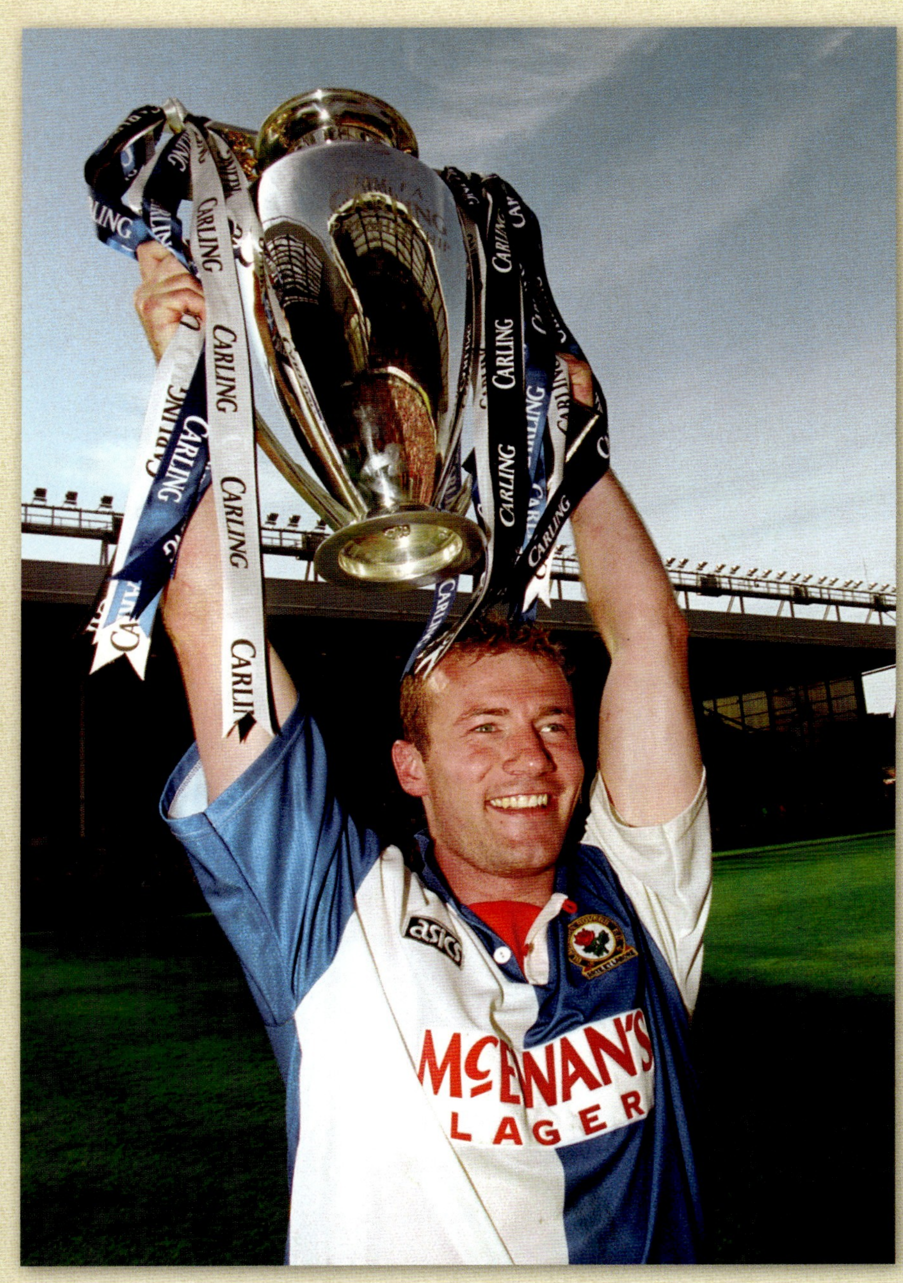

BLACKBURN ROVERS' ALAN SHEARER CELEBRATES WITH THE CARLING PREMIERSHIP TROPHY. 14/05/1995

ERIC CANTONA OF MANCHESTER UNITED (L) CELEBRATES WITH TEAMMATE ROY KEANE (R) AFTER SCORING FROM THE PENALTY SPOT AGAINST LIVERPOOL ON HIS RETURN TO SOCCER AFTER A NINE MONTH SUSPENSION. 01/10/1995

ENGLAND GOALKEEPER DAVID SEAMAN CELEBRATES AFTER SAVING A PENALTY FROM SPAIN'S MIGUEL ANGEL NADAL, WHICH PUT ENGLAND THROUGH TO THE SEMI FINALS OF EURO 96. 22/06/1996

ENGLAND'S STUART PEARCE EXORCISES THE GHOSTS OF PENALTIES PAST AS HE CELEBRATES AFTER SCORING IN THE PENALTY SHOOT-OUT TO DECIDE THE EURO 96 QUARTER FINAL CLASH AGAINST SPAIN, AT WEMBLEY. 22/06/1996

BARNSLEY'S JOHN HENDRIE IS LIFTED ALOFT AT THE FINAL WHISTLE AS HIS TEAM CLINCH PROMOTION. 26/04/1997

ENGLAND'S MICHAEL OWEN (R) AND DAVID BECKHAM (L) CELEBRATE OWEN'S EQUALISING GOAL IN THE WORLD CUP GAME AGAINST ROMANIA. 22/06/1998

ENGLAND'S DAVID BECKHAM (R) IS SHOWN THE RED CARD BY REFEREE KIM MILTON NIELSEN (L) IN THE WORLD CUP SECOND ROUND MATCH AGAINST ARGENTINA. 30/06/1998

WIGAN ATHLETIC'S WINNING GOALSCORER PAUL ROGERS IS THE VICTIM OF A PRACTICAL JOKE AS HE CELEBRATES WITH THE AUTO WINDSCREENS SHIELD. 18/04/1999

MICHAEL OWEN (ON FLOOR) AND THE LIVERPOOL FANS CAN'T BELIEVE THEIR LUCK AS MANCHESTER UNITED GOALKEEPER MASSIMO TAIBI KEEPS ANOTHER SHOT OUT DURING AN FA PREMIERSHIP MATCH. 11/09/1999

ENGLAND CAPTAIN DAVID BECKHAM (FRONT) CELEBRATES WITH TEAMMATE EMILE HESKEY AFTER SCORING THE EQUALISER FROM A FREE KICK AGAINST GREECE IN THE DYING SECONDS OF THE WORLD CUP EUROPEAN QUALIFYING GROUP NINE MATCH AT OLD TRAFFORD. 06/10/2001

ENGLAND'S DAVID BECKHAM (L) CELEBRATES WITH TREVOR SINCLAIR (R) AFTER SCORING THE WINNING GOAL FROM A PENALTY KICK AGAINST ARGENTINA IN A WORLD CUP GROUP F MATCH. 07/06/2002

OPPOSITE

LIVERPOOL CAPTAIN STEVEN GERRARD TAKES A MOMENT TO REFLECT ON HIS TEAM'S DRAMATIC COMEBACK AGAINST AC MILAN ENSURING THE UEFA CHAMPIONS LEAGUE TROPHY STAYS IN LIVERPOOL. 25/05/2005

ENGLAND'S WAYNE ROONEY IS SENT OFF DURING THE WORLD CUP QUARTER FINAL FOR A FOUL ON PORTUGAL'S ALBERTO RICARDO CARVALHO. 01/07/2006

CELTIC CAPTAIN NEIL LENNON HOLDS THE BANK OF SCOTLAND SCOTTISH PREMIER LEAGUE TROPHY.
29/04/2007

The Publishers gratefully acknowledge PA Photos, from whose extensive archive – including The Press Association, Barratts and Sport & General collections – the photographs in this book have been selected.

Personal copies of the photographs in this book, and many others, may be ordered online at www.prints.paphotos.com

For more information, please contact:

AMMONITE PRESS

AE Publications Ltd. 166 High Street, Lewes, East Sussex, BN7 1XU, United Kingdom

Tel: 01273 488005 Fax: 01273 402866

www.ae-publications.com